Spiritual INVESTMENTS

Money is like love;
it kills slowly and painfully
the one who withholds it,
and enlivens the other who
turns it on his fellow man.

—Kahlil Gibran

Spiritual INVESTMENTS

WALL STREET WISDOM
from the Career of
SIR JOHN TEMPLETON

Gary Moore

Templeton Foundation Press
Philadelphia & London

TEMPLETON FOUNDATION PRESS
Five Radnor Corporate Center, Suite 120
100 Matsonford Road
Radnor, Pennsylvania 19087

Library of Congress Cataloging-in-Publication Data

Moore, Gary D.
    Spiritual Investments: Wall Street wisdom from the career of
Sir John Templeton / Gary Moore.
        p.   cm.
    ISBN 1-890151-18-1 (hc. : alk. paper)
    1. Templeton, John, 1912–   . 2. Capitalists and financiers—
United States. 3. Investments, American. 4. Finance, Personal—
Religious aspects. I. Title.
HG172.T45M66   1998
332.6'092—dc21
[b]   98-38607
                                                                 CIP

Special thanks to Michelle Gorman, research associate
Designed by Helene Krasney

"Madras Muslin" pattern used on dust jacket and in book is by
William Morris; courtesy of the Trustees of the V & A
(Victoria and Albert Museum, London).

Contents

INTRODUCTION

*Ethics and spiritual principles should be the
basis of everything we do in life. All that we say. All
that we think. Every activity should be based on
that—including the selection of investments.*
—Sir John Templeton

A decade ago, I was a senior vice president of investments with Paine Webber. Then I discovered that Wall Street alone could not offer true success or real happiness. I thought of attending seminary. Near the end of the year-long process of peer reviews, psychological testing, and spiritual retreats, each aspirant was asked to name his mentor in the business world. I had never thought about it before. But after a few seconds of reflection, I announced that my mentor would have to be Sir John Templeton.

I never went to seminary. Encouraged to develop my skills in an area where I showed at least modest promise, I began a closer friendship with Sir John. This association has resulted in my serving as an advisor to his foundation and writing about the "riches" he has shared with me over the years.*

The Wealth of the World, the Riches of the Spirit

Many investors hold their breath as they await Sir John's views on the health of the stock market or the next commodity that might soar in value. And he often accommodates them with astute financial

---

*This book contains a few nuggets of those riches; a more comprehensive discussion is presented in my book: *Ten Golden Rules for Financial Success: Riches I've Gathered from Legendary Mutual Fund Manager Sir John M. Templeton*. Grand Rapids, Michigan: ZondervanPublishingHouse, *a Division* of HarperCollins *Publishers*, 1996.

predictions. But Sir John also shares spiritual wisdom that can enrich them in other ways. Investors may be surprised by this, but it is Sir John's ability to combine financial discernment and spiritual insights that has made him the legendary financial leader that he is.

Appearing beneath the headline "Sir John Templeton: How to Beat the Market" on the January 16, 1995 cover of *Forbes* was this statement from Sir John: "Wrong question: Where is the outlook good? Right question: Where is it miserable?" In the article, he said "the time to buy is at the point of maximum pessimism." Sir John says that most problems will be remedied.

But he also has the courage to act on that faith. Believing one thing but doing another is considered by many of the world's cultures to be a characteristic of the "lower nature of human beings." Sir John's position is that it is what we do, not merely what we believe, that determines our success in investments and in life. Although most investors say they believe in his "contrarian" approach to investing (discipline and patience rather than reaction and panic), market research has recently shown that mutual fund investors realize only about one-half of the returns generated by public mutual funds. The reason? Most people tend to buy when things look promising and sell when things look ominous.

As useful as price/earnings ratios, book values, and dozens of other indicators have been to Sir John over the years, investors typically ignore them at crucial decision points as they become caught up in either euphoria or the fear of loss. But the essence of Sir John's philosophy is that, to achieve success, investors can transcend such human tendencies through spiritual development. That he has been one of the best-performing and well-respected mutual fund managers in the world over the past half-century is evidence of the success of Sir John's philosophy. It is this philosophy that infuses this book and will inspire its readers.

A Global Perspective, a Prophetic Vision

In the early years of the Templeton Growth Fund, Sir John invested in Japanese companies, contrary to the prevailing practices and mood of this post-World War II era. Japan's political and economic infrastructures were in shambles. For decades, the phrase "Made in Japan" would be associated with cheap trinkets. Seeing beyond these temporary material conditions, Sir John recognized the Japanese as a people infused with an ancient spirit of thrift, hard work, family values, and company loyalties.

Proving the value of his global perspective, Sir John has practiced his investment philosophy all over the world, even when nations have grown dispirited by their own troubled economies. He began to make what turned out to be prophetic market observations. For example, when the Dow Jones Industrial Average stood at 172 in March 1949, he wrote, "When we look back ten years from now, 172 will probably appear to be a bargain level." Ten years later, the Dow was above 600.

In 1982, John made a famous statement to Louis Rukeyser, host of the television show *Wall $treet Week*: "The Dow may triple from the 1,000 level to the 3,000 level by 1990." That same year, I wrote an article for the *New York Times* newspaper group that advanced John's belief. With the benefit of hindsight, this now seems almost unremarkable.

But at the time, Americans were very skeptical of this perspective. Some of my clients even thought I had lost my mind and went elsewhere. And I couldn't blame them. The prime rate had risen to 21%. America seemed hostage to the Organization of Petroleum Exporting Countries (OPEC). And Japan was no longer selling inexpensive trinkets, but high-quality automobiles and televisions.

Yet the Dow did rise to the 3,000 level by 1990. John again appeared on *Wall $treet Week* and predicted that it "might rise to 6,000 and perhaps much more" by the year 2000. He predicted that our world would be entering the "twenty most prosperous years in history" because of the collapse of communism and the Berlin Wall. Again, that seems obvious in retrospect.

But it was anything but obvious at the time. Americans were dispirited by the recession, and the federal debt shaped our pessimistic economic perceptions. Best-selling books about another "great depression" in 1990, an economic earthquake in 1992, and bankruptcy in 1995 lined the shelves of both secular and religious bookstores. An American president lost the White House because of our perceptions of the U.S. economy.

Our $5 trillion federal liability is well known. Yet for years, the Office of Management and Budget (OMB) has estimated our national assets (fiscal and human capital) at $55 trillion, and our annual gross national product at more than $7 trillion. Why is it that no one seems to have looked at the positive side of America's balance sheet? Such misperception, largely shaped by the media, is one of the major challenges that Sir John says investors must transcend.

During the early nineties, Sir John was counting our blessings, not our problems. In 1991, he invested a higher percentage of his funds' assets in American stocks than at any time in his career. His vision was again rewarded. As I write, the Dow has soared beyond the 9,000 level. Americans in 1998 seem euphoric about the economy, and the spirit of plenty is evident in our expectations of the market.

But in 1998, Sir John has again advised us to invest abroad, especially in Asia, despite the prevailing mood of pessimism there. Many grumble that he is pulling investment dollars away from the New America, where "this time is different"—a phrase that Sir John calls the "four most costly words in the English language."

Additional Insights

Before we get to my summaries of the spiritual principles that Sir John has generously shared over the decades, let me offer just a few more of the investment and life principles that Sir John has abided by but might never talk about himself. His methods teach us that we are investing not only in economies, but in human beings. *Therefore, we should invest with a spirit of:*

✒ *Love.* North America continues to dominate the world's economy. Our stock, bond, real estate, and money markets are deeper and more liquid than any in history. And Americans tend to be somewhat nationalistic in their investment practices. But Sir John maintains that we should operate from a spirit of love for all humankind, investing at least a portion of our assets in less economically developed nations.

During America's last great bear market from 1968 to 1974, prominent money managers lost 50% or more of their assets because they invested solely in domestic stocks, while Sir John prospered by diversifying his investments around the world. He recognized that preparing for economic cycles, which have been with us since the seven fat years and seven lean years of ancient Egypt, can be enriching.

Perseverance. Much of what we know about the benefits of global diversification comes from Sir John's perseverance. Early in his career as a fund manager, today's legendary financial leader managed the Templeton Growth Fund from an obscure, tiny office above a branch of the Nassau police department. In those days, most North Americans were skeptical of mutual funds and virtually never thought about international investments. It took the "Dean of Global Investing" decades to convince us of the merits of a mutual fund that invests in all of humankind.

 Patience. The first rule of *making* money is not to *lose* it. The second rule is to never forget the first rule! The typical American mutual fund manager now trades, rather than holds onto, most of our stocks each year—and our bonds even faster. While Sir John has never been one to criticize his contemporaries, he has held his stocks four to five times longer than the typical fund manager. Studies consistently show that, as a group, mutual fund managers who invest rather than trade make more money with lower risks and fewer taxes.

For example, Fund A has a history of making 100% one year but losing 50% the next. Fund B makes only 10% in up markets but stays even in down markets. But Fund B will actually produce greater long-term rewards. The only reason to consider Fund A is if you can "time" the market, something Sir John says very few investors can accomplish in the long run.

❧ *Ethics.* Having "ethics" means not only doing the *right* thing, but doing the *smart* thing. Despite most Wall Street teachings, Sir John maintains that ethics *enhance* an investor's long-term returns rather than *hinder* them.

When he was managing the Templeton funds, Sir John made it a policy to generally avoid what brokers call the "sin stocks" of alcohol, tobacco, and gambling companies, a policy that the funds still follow today. Sir John says it is "only common sense, which is why it isn't common" that investors avoid companies that governments, physicians, and other activists are trying to restrict because of their negative "contributions" to society and invest in companies that are beneficial to ourselves and to our neighbors.

Wholeness. Finally, Sir John would tell you that the spiritual principles you are about to learn will not only enhance your investing, but your relationships, your career, and, in fact, every aspect of your life. This is especially true if you are engaged in what he calls the "ministry of business." Like the Protestant reformers of centuries ago, Sir John tells us that our daily vocations are definite and beneficial forms of ministry:

> If you select the true spiritual principles . . . you'll have more customers. Your business will grow. . . . If you try to operate a business without spiritual principles, it will not last long, and you will not do much good in the world.

Like Mother Teresa, one can do "good" without receiving—or wanting—material reward. But doing "good" is how investors and business people do "well," paving their road to financial success on a solid foundation of spiritual and humanitarian principles. This is never an easy road to traverse. But the track record of the Templeton funds is proof that it is a far surer path than the one chosen by many investors in recent decades.

And Sir John Templeton's journey from a poor lad in the hills of Tennessee to one of the world's wealthiest—and "richest"—men is proof that it is a road that can lead us to life's true rewards.

1. Invest for maximum total real return.

FINANCIAL PRINCIPLE

To clearly evaluate an investment, we need to look at the return after taxes and inflation. This is the most rational objective for long-term investors. Any investment strategy that disregards the insidious effect of taxes and inflation fails to recognize the true nature of the economic environment.

Protecting the purchasing power of investments is vital to maintaining a strong portfolio. One of the biggest mistakes investors make is putting too much money into fixed-income securities and failing to factor into their formula the fluctuating value of world currencies, which normally results in rising consumer prices.

Invest for maximum total real return.

For example, if inflation averages 4% a year, it will reduce the buying power of a $100,000 portfolio to $68,000 in just ten years. In other words, to maintain the same buying power, that portfolio would have to grow to $147,000 dollars—a 47% gain simply to maintain its value over a decade. And this does not even take into consideration the effect of taxes.

Look at the whole economic picture
when evaluating an investment.

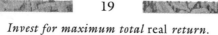

Invest for maximum total real *return.*

SPIRITUAL PRINCIPLE

Learning discernment is an important step in becoming more responsible and spiritual in our outlook toward life. We can learn to evaluate the essential aspects of all situations to determine whether we are making the best possible choice, whether it be a job, a relationship, or a spiritual path. To do this, we learn to take a panoramic view of the whole situation, not just the part that might be easiest to deal with.

Sometimes, the easiest path to take might be the one that appears the safest. But the easiest and safest paths are not always the most fruitful courses or highest roads we can take in life. In fact, as we make choices, we often project our fears or

Invest for maximum total real return.

desires onto the issues at hand. Developing the power of discernment means that we can look objectively at life decisions and choose freely.

Therefore, as we look at the big picture, we can make sound choices and not allow ourselves to be led down the safest or easiest path simply to avoid challenges or fear.

> *Discernment with proper perspective is the foundation of honesty, responsibility, and wise choices.*

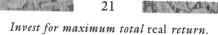

Invest for maximum total real *return.*

2. Invest—
don't trade
or speculate.

FINANCIAL PRINCIPLE

When deciding how to handle our portfolios, we should keep in mind the wise words of Lucien O. Hooper, a Wall Street Legend: "What always impresses me," he wrote, "is how much better the relaxed, long-term owners of stock do with their portfolios than the traders do with their switching of inventory. The relaxed investor is usually better informed and more understanding of essential values; he is more patient and less emotional; he pays smaller annual capital gains taxes; he does not incur unnecessary brokerage commissions; and he avoids behaving like Cassius by 'thinking too much.' "

We do better in the long run by viewing the stock market as a "home base," rather than as a

Invest—don't trade or speculate.

trip to the casino. If we trade stocks every time they move a point or two, continually sell short, deal only in options, or trade in futures, our dreams of a big win may mask our increased risk of eventual—or even frequent—loss.

Also, profits may be consumed by commissions, or a market expected to turn down may go up—in defiance of careful calculations and short sales. If a Wall Street news announcer says, "This just in," our hearts will stop; we will devote far more energy than necessary to make our portfolios successful.

Maintaining constancy in investments will prove the most rewarding strategy.

Invest—don't trade or speculate.

SPIRITUAL PRINCIPLE

It is important to think of your commitments in life as long-term investments. You will get a lot more out of your life's endeavors if you are as constant as possible. Invest your talents, energy, and emotion in your work, relationships, and spiritual life. Do it wisely and with careful forethought and planning, and try to stay with your commitments for the long-haul. You will find that you get a greater return with less personal expenditure.

If you are able to calm your mind and stay relaxed as you pursue your life's goals, you will find them to be far more obtainable. Constantly jumping from one ideology, relationship, or

Invest—don't trade or speculate.

commitment to another takes a toll on one's emotions and well-being—which is not to say that you should stay in a bad situation just to maintain your investment. But staying with the ethical and moral choices that you have made in your life is more productive and less draining than backtracking and starting from scratch, over and over again.

Maintaining constancy based on wisdom while pursuing life's goals brings peace of mind and eventual rewards.

Invest—don't trade or speculate.

*3. Remain flexible
and open-minded about
types of investments.*

FINANCIAL PRINCIPLE

One of the facts of investing is that no one kind of investment is always best. To create a successful portfolio, it is crucial to keep an open mind about types of investments. There are times to buy blue chip stocks, cyclical stocks, corporate bonds, convertible bonds, U.S. treasury instruments, and so on. And then there are times to sit on cash and treasury bills, because they can enable you to take advantage of investment opportunities.

If a particular industry or type of security becomes popular with investors, that popularity will always prove temporary and, when lost, may not return for many years. Don't look to popular

Remain flexible and open-minded about types of investments.

trends to direct you toward the best investment opportunities. You can have no real safety without preserving your purchasing power.

If you keep your eyes and mind open, you will have far greater success than the investor who is locked into certain types of investment opportunities.

Remaining flexible as an investor, improves your chances of developing a diversified and rewarding portfolio.

Remain flexible and open-minded about types of investments.

SPIRITUAL PRINCIPLE

Life's many twists and turns require that we be flexible. Every day can bring with it new options, demands, and invitations, but we can benefit from them only if we are willing to be exposed to their presence. If we open our minds to the many situations that present themselves to us, we can learn to grow and expand our boundaries.

The nature of the universe is that not everything is simple for us to understand or predict. Part of humility is accepting our limited ability to foresee what the universe has in store for us, remaining open to the challenges and opportunities that will manifest themselves as we go along.

Remain flexible and open-minded about types of investments.

Being closed to the possibilities that lie before us will limit our horizons.

Belief and conviction do not have to be obstacles to pursuing new prospects. There is a difference between being resolute in one's beliefs and convictions and being obstinately opposed to any kind of change. Sometimes the directions that our lives are intended to take are not obvious—but we will never see them if we close our eyes, hearts, and minds.

Remaining open to the variety of life's riches
brings opportunities for personal
and spiritual growth.

Remain flexible and open-minded about types of investments.

4. Buy low—
at the point of
maximum pessimism.

FINANCIAL PRINCIPLE

Every investor knows to buy low. But in actual practice, this isn't the way the market works. When prices are high, demand is high. When prices are low, demand is low—investors have pulled back, and people are discouraged.

When almost everyone is pessimistic at the same time, a further market collapse is a rare event. More often, stocks in only particular fields fall. Industries such as automaking and casualty insurance go through regular cycles, or occasionally stocks of certain types of companies, such as thrift institutions, fall out of favor all at once.

Investors on the sidelines might be advising to buy low and sell high; but all too many of them

Buy low—at the point of maximum pessimism.

buy high and sell low. Sure, they will buy—but only after analysts agree on a favorable outlook. This is foolish, but it's human nature.

It is extremely difficult to go against the crowd, to buy when everyone else is selling, when things look darkest. And if we buy with the crowd, we will achieve the same results as everyone else. By definition, we can't outperform the market if we buy the market. Bernard Baruch, adviser to presidents, put this principle most succinctly when he said, "Never follow the crowd."

Investment decisions contrary to "conventional wisdom" can be the most rewarding.

Buy low—at the point of maximum pessimism.

Spiritual Principle

Sometimes, the dark places in our lives can actually be sources of light and optimism. Just as falling stocks often have unseen value that can be missed, so, too, people who seem to be at their lowest point have innate goodness and potential that may go unrecognized. Seeing that value and investing time, trust, and attention in those (including ourselves) who "hit bottom" can bring rich rewards.

From the bottom, it is possible to see only up—things can only get better. No matter what catastrophes or dilemmas we experience, we can turn our lives around through the help of friends, hard work, service, and faith. Indeed, people who hit bottom often become the greatest success

Buy low—at the point of maximum pessimism.

stories. And they often are more deeply appreciative of and grateful for their successes than are those to whom things have come easily.

Investing in humanity is always a worthwhile endeavor; but investing in ourselves or others in times of trouble is not only the humane course of action, but an investment that will likely bring high personal and spiritual dividends for ourselves and those we help.

Having the faith to invest in humanity in times of trouble shows that great change and growth can come from the lowest points in life.

Buy low—at the point of maximum pessimism.

*5. Search
for quality
when buying.*

FINANCIAL PRINCIPLE

When investing, search for bargains among quality stocks. A bargain is no bargain if you've bought an inferior stock.

Quality is a company that's strongly entrenched as the sales leader in a growing market. *Quality* is a company that's the technological leader in a field that depends on technical innovation. *Quality* is a strong management team with a proven track record. *Quality* is being the low-cost producer in an industry. *Quality* is a well-capitalized company that is among the first to enter a new market. *Quality* is a well-known, trusted brand of high-profit-margin consumer product.

Search for quality when buying.

You cannot consider these attributes in isolation. A company may be a low-cost producer, but its product line may also be falling out of favor. Or, the technological leader in a field may not have adequate capital for expansion.

Determining quality in a stock is like reviewing a restaurant: It needs to be truly superior before it gets that fourth star. And your ability to determine quality in stocks will grow as your research and investment experience expands.

A "bargain" is not necessarily a good investment—it must also demonstrate quality.

Search for quality when buying.

SPIRITUAL PRINCIPLE

Surrounding yourself with quality people can help you grow as a person. On the other hand, there is that old saying about associating with people of bad character: "If you lie down with dogs, you will wake up with fleas."

The character of your friends and associates has an impact on your own character development. Constantly look for ways to grow and become a better person. Associate with people whose actions and beliefs you respect and admire.

Discerning quality in people is not always easy. Make sure you are not taken in by "bargain" relationships, the kind that are easy to come by but end up costing you more in the long run. In

Search for quality when buying.

fact, choosing quality is a skill that requires fine-tuning as you clarify your life objectives. As you determine the qualities you seek for yourself, you will naturally be drawn to people whose qualities you admire in turn. You can learn from each other in a mutually supportive way.

Avoid "bargain relationships";
associate with people of high spiritual and moral
quality—they can help you become
the person you choose to be.

Search for quality when buying.

6. Buy value,
not market trends or
economic outlook.

FINANCIAL PRINCIPLE

Buy real value in stocks. Do not be influenced by market trends or economic outlook. A wise investor knows that the stock market is really a "market of stocks." While individual stocks may be pulled along momentarily by a strong bull market, ultimately it is the individual stocks that determine the market, not vice versa. If investors focus only on market trends or economic outlook, they may not realize that individual stocks can rise in a bear market and fall in a bull market.

Value is inherent in each individual stock and varies considerably among investment opportunities. The stock market and the economy do not always march in lockstep. Bear markets do not

Buy value, not market trends or economic outlook.

always coincide with recessions, and an overall decline in corporate earnings does not always cause a simultaneous decline in stock prices.

You can determine your investment success
by seeking and finding value in individual stocks
rather than by being misled by market
trends or economic outlook.

Buy value, not market trends or economic outlook.

SPIRITUAL PRINCIPLE

We often criticize or prejudge situations and people unfairly. But if we look at actual circumstances and avoid being persuaded by the opinions of others, we can better assess the value that may be hidden in a situation or a person.

Make your life decisions based on your own clear assessments, not on popular trends. Again, don't follow the crowd as you weave your way through life. The crowd does not always make the best decisions, and they often are not thinking about the highest good when making them.

We can learn to make better choices in life and achieve a better appreciation of people if we take the time to look beyond trends and superficial

Buy value, not market trends or economic outlook.

opinion. To experience the value in a situation or person requires more than a knowledge of general opinion. It requires an attempt to gather information, grasp nuances and subtleties, and have the courage to make up our own minds.

When making choices, especially regarding the people you wish to include in your life, rely on your own perceptions; do not be influenced by the opinions of others.

Buy value, not market trends or economic outlook.

7. Diversify.

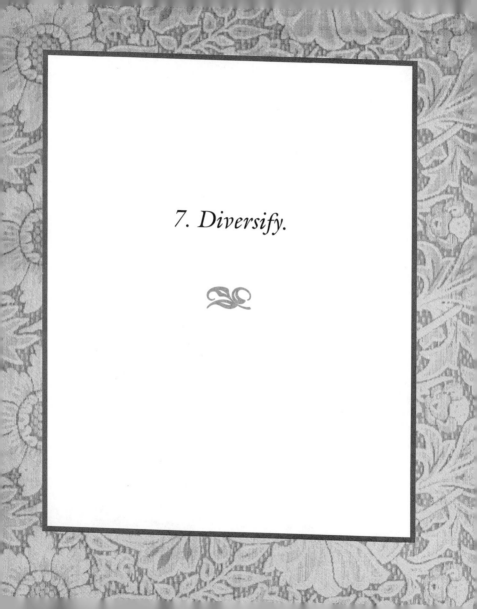

Financial Principle

In stocks and bonds, as in many other aspects of life, you find greater safety in numbers. No matter how careful you are, no matter how much research you do, you can neither predict nor control the future. A hurricane or earthquake, a strike at a supplier, an unexpected technological advance by a competitor, a government-ordered product recall, or serious internal problems—any one of these can cost you millions of dollars.

To protect yourself against inevitable problems in any one area of your portfolio, you must diversify. By company, by industry, by risk, and by country, you must spread out your investment dollars. Cast a wide net, and you will reap the

Diversify.

benefits of your efforts. For example, if you search worldwide, you will find more and possibly better bargains than are possible to find in any single nation's economic system.

But don't be fooled into thinking that diversifying will be an easy task. It takes research and work to ensure that you are making wise investments in areas with which you may be unfamiliar. But the advantages that come with diversifying will more than reward your endeavors.

Balancing your portfolio by diversifying will protect and enhance your investments.

Diversify.

SPIRITUAL PRINCIPLE

People who only work, only play, only complain, miss out on the benefits of a more diversified approach to life. If you study a particular subject to the exclusion of all others, you will not be truly educated.

The same is true for anything you pursue. If you dedicate your energies to only one facet of life to the exclusion of everything else, you precariously place your energy in only one area without realizing the variety of joys life has to offer.

If you lose that basket into which you've placed all your eggs, you have little left to value. People who pursue multiple interests—the professor who does woodworking on the weekend, the physicist

Diversify.

who reads theology daily, the carpenter who attends Shakespearean festivals in the summer— will find their lives richer.

Life's rewards do not come from devoting your energies to a single cause or pursuit. Balance and diversified interests—family, friends, vocation, spiritual life, arts, and recreation—create a more fulfilling existence and a more complete person. Incorporating the lessons learned from one aspect of life into others helps to create wisdom.

Investing your energy in life's
diversified riches reaps great rewards.

Diversify.

8. Do your homework or hire reliable experts to help you.

FINANCIAL PRINCIPLE

Obtain sound information to make the best investment decisions. Listen to those who tell you to "investigate before you invest." Study various companies to learn what makes them successful. Exercise diligence before you make choices. And hire experts to help you turn your portfolio's performance from middling to outstanding.

Remember, in most instances you are buying either earnings or assets. In free-enterprise nations, earnings and assets together are major influences on the price of most stocks. The earnings on stock market indexes—whether it be Dow Jones, NASDAQ, or any other—fluctuate around the replacement book value of the shares of the

Do your homework or hire experts to help you.

index. If you expect a company to grow, you are buying future earnings. If you expect a company to be acquired or dissolved at a premium over its market price, you are buying assets.

It is important for you to have all information necessary to be able to separate the wheat from the chaff.

Whether you do the research yourself or hire experts to assist you, developing a strong knowledge base will allow you to make wise choices.

Do your homework or hire experts to help you.

SPIRITUAL PRINCIPLE

Research, plan, analyze. Learning to look before you leap will not stop you from enjoying life, but will help you avoid unnecessary worry. There is something to be said for spontaneity—it certainly adds spice and a bit of the unexpected to life. But for major life decisions, doing some preplanning is not only helpful, but essential. You cannot know what curves life is going to throw you, but you can prepare for many eventualities by arming yourself with good information.

If you are uncertain of your abilities to analyze a situation fully or accurately, do not be afraid or embarrassed to seek the advice of experts. Acknowledging that you are not omnipotent is

Do your homework or hire experts to help you.

not a sign of weakness. Knowing your resources—gleaning the wisdom of those more experienced or educated—can guide you in your more difficult decisions. And accepting this wisdom will make you a better person.

Pride can be a terrible foe if it prevents us from getting the support or guidance we need.

Making decisions based on study, reflection, and seeking help from others can help you make wise choices in life.

Do your homework or hire experts to help you.

9. Monitor

your

investments.

FINANCIAL PRINCIPLE

Keep alert, and aggressively monitor your investments. No bull market is permanent, no bear market is permanent. No stock is a sure thing, and there are no stocks that you can just buy and forget about. The pace of change is great, and investors must expect and react appropriately to it.

To act in your own best interests, you must be prepared, informed, and watchful of your investments. Complacency opens the door to surprise and disappointment. You must always be ready to cope with the changes that will confront you.

Consider the changes affecting the Dow Jones Industrials or the shifts that occur in companies on Fortune's 100 largest industrials list.

Monitor your investments.

Bankruptcies, acquisitions, mergers, and privatizations occur regularly, without much warning.

In today's litigious world, one significant class-action lawsuit can bring an otherwise successful company to its knees. Governments topple with regularity as the world adjusts to ever-changing political forces. So—with the rare exception of a truly professional fund manager or investment counselor—don't assume that others will keep watch for you. No one else has as much interest in your investments as you do.

Wise investors continually look for signs of change and stay informed to protect their investments.

Monitor your investments.

SPIRITUAL PRINCIPLE

We cannot predict all change in our lives, nor can we anticipate our reactions to the challenges we are forced to confront. Our world, no matter how we seek to stabilize it, is in a constant state of flux, and we must adapt along with it, oftentimes with very little time for preparation or reflection. We must, therefore, be ever vigilant.

This level of vigilance requires a constant reappraisal of one's character. Heraclitus once said, "Man's fate is his character." We write our own fate as we assess, evaluate, and seek to improve ourselves in preparation for what might come.

Our ability to be prepared for the challenges we will face in our daily lives is linked to our

Monitor your investments.

spiritual strength. Even though we cannot determine what will happen in the world around us, we can ensure that we are spiritually ready to take on any development in our lives by honestly taking stock of our spiritual assets and personal flaws—and working to improve both.

Ask yourself what is important to you. Where are you going? What can you do to make the world a better place along the way?

Taking personal inventory and monitoring your spiritual assets helps you to successfully adapt to life's changes.

Monitor your investments.

10. Don't panic.

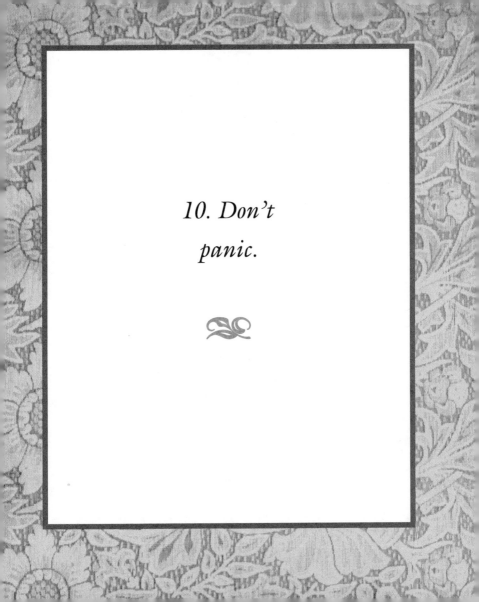

FINANCIAL PRINCIPLE

In times of greatest economic stress, the worst thing you can do as an investor is to panic. Reactions to situations that are born of fear are rarely wise or helpful. Perhaps you didn't sell before everyone else began to, and you're caught in a market slump, such as the one we had in 1987. There you are, facing a huge loss, all in one day. Your first instinct may very well be to call your broker and sell as quickly as you can. This is a classic panic reaction.

Don't allow yourself to give into that initial panic attack; don't rush to sell the next day. The time to sell is *before* the crash, not after. Instead, take a deep breath, and study your portfolio. If you

Don't panic.

didn't own these stocks now, would you buy them after the market crash? Chances are that you would; they'd be even cheaper. Selling them would not be a correction, but a reaction.

The only reason to sell after the crash would be to buy other, more attractive stocks. But it is unlikely that other stocks would be more appealing than those you already have. If your portfolio performed well before the crash, believe in the instincts you used to build it.

In the face of a financial crisis, evaluate your portfolio and hold onto it; don't panic and sell unless you find something likely to be more beneficial.

Don't panic.

SPIRITUAL PRINCIPLE

Everyone is faced with challenges and times of crisis in life. It is during these times that it becomes most important to rely on faith. Relax, breathe. Fear paralyzes us into a state of inaction or, even worse, makes us react to crisis without thinking first. Take stock of yourself, allow yourself the time to evaluate the reality of the whole situation within the scope of historical changes.

If you give yourself the opportunity to assess a crisis from a position of faith, you will find yourself able to move past the panic stage and take appropriate action.

If you still find yourself filled with panic, evaluate your faith. Fear and faith do not coexist. Faith

Don't panic.

in the power of the universe dispels panic. Force yourself to remember the strength that has guided you through difficult times in the past, and allow yourself to rely on the conviction that there is a higher power—God or however you construe it—to get you past whatever fears are confronting you.

As we move through life and face challenges head on, we must be confident in our spiritual center to be able to address crises from a position of strength, not trepidation.

In the face of a personal crisis, evaluate your faith and hold onto it—it is the antidote to fear.

Don't panic.

11. Learn from your mistakes.

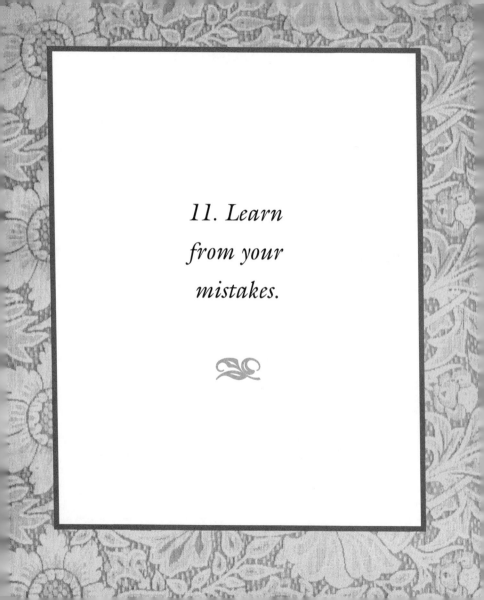

FINANCIAL PRINCIPLE

The only way to avoid mistakes is not to invest, which is probably the biggest mistake of all. So forgive yourself for your errors. Don't allow yourself to become discouraged, and certainly don't try to recoup your losses by taking bigger risks. Instead, turn each mistake into a learning experience. Determine exactly what went wrong and how you can avoid the same mistake in the future.

The investor who says, "this time is different," when in fact it is virtually a repeat of an earlier situation, has uttered the four costliest words in the language of investing. You cannot change a situation without making a full appraisal of your role in what went wrong.

Learn from your mistakes.

Taking responsibility for mistakes can be more rewarding than taking credit for successes.

Mistakes are a natural consequence of action. Do not associate mistakes with failure. If everyone who made mistakes in investing were considered a failure, no one would ever become a success. Even Sir John has acknowledged that one-third of his investments prove unwise; but the other two-thirds bring him great rewards.

The biggest difference between investors who are successful and those who are not is that the former acknowledge—and learn from—their mistakes.

Learn from your mistakes.

SPIRITUAL PRINCIPLE

To err is human. Sometimes our human propensity to make mistakes is a truth that is hard to accept. We may aim for excellence, and that is a noble and worthwhile goal. But perfection is simply not attainable, and is often an excuse not to try.

Our fear of making mistakes, if not tempered by an understanding of the value of their lessons, can be quite paralyzing. If we are immobilized by a preoccupation with what could potentially go wrong, we will never give ourselves the opportunity to go forward, try new things, invent, create.

Accept that mistakes come with all endeavors. The greatest mistake is not to participate, not to

Learn from your mistakes.

engage in life. Take each mistake and analyze it fully. Understand its origin, and make its lesson a part of your future actions, choices, and decisions.

Would humanity have achieved all that it has in the last century without trial and error? The Wright brothers crashed more than they flew, but each crash produced new information that led to the right formula for making man airborne. Shoot for success, certainly—but don't let setbacks deter you from your goals.

Progress in life is built on the lessons learned from human error.

Learn from your mistakes.

*12. Use prayer to
gain perspective
and quiet your mind.*

FINANCIAL PRINCIPLE

If we begin with prayer, we can think more clearly and make fewer mistakes. Confusion is one of the investor's greatest foes. And it is easy to become increasingly confused in today's marketplace as investment information is "commoditized" in the media. So many options and so much information is at our disposal.

Years ago, investing was a much more straightforward enterprise. Today, it takes more than information and know-how to be successful in the competitive world of investments. We must differentiate knowledge and wisdom.

Also, investing should not be about just the bottom line. The secret of creating riches for

Use prayer to gain perspective and quiet your mind.

ourselves is to create them for others. If investors shun the "Midas" attitude, their wealth can exert a positive force.

Stewardship, the belief that what you have is not actually yours, but is held in trust for the good of humanity, is an important foundation of good investment. Prayer can lead us to that belief.

The serenity that comes with prayer
can cut through confusion when making
investment decisions.

Use prayer to gain perspective and quiet your mind.

SPIRITUAL PRINCIPLE

When life seems uncontrollable, or your mind or spirit is uneasy, use prayer to find your center again. The quietude and solace found in prayer can be found nowhere else in like measure. Prayer comes from within. When we pray, we are required to shut out the world around us, thereby affording us an opportunity to focus our energies.

It is wise to begin any new task or endeavor with prayer. Prayer can open the mind to options or avenues that might not otherwise be apparent to us. It can clear the mind of the haze and confusion that we often experience as a result of everyday issues.

Use prayer to gain perspective and quiet your mind.

Grounding ourselves through prayer when life presents its most difficult challenges will afford greater strength and patience. Our prayers may not always be answered in the way we would like, but the simple act of prayer, of asking for guidance, calms the spirit. From that calm can spring wonderful new ideas and solutions. Quite often, the answers come when we're still enough to ask the right questions.

Use prayer to aim for the highest good when making any life decisions.

Use prayer to gain perspective and quiet your mind.

*13. Recognize
the difficulty of
outperforming
the market.*

FINANCIAL PRINCIPLE

The challenge to outperforming the market is not simply making better investment decisions than the average investor. The *real* challenge is making investment decisions that are better than those of the professionals who manage the big institutions.

Remember, the unmanaged market indexes, such as Standard & Poor's 500, don't pay commissions to buy and sell stock. They have no need to consider the risks of investing. They don't pay salaries to security analysts or portfolio managers. And, unlike the unmanaged indexes, investment companies are never 100% invested because they need to have cash on hand to redeem shares.

Recognize the difficulty of outperforming the market.

So, any investment company that consistently outperforms the market is actually doing a much better job than you might think. And if it does so by a significant degree, it is doing a superb job.

Outperforming the market is an ambitious goal, and one that must be pursued carefully.

Recognize the difficulty of outperforming the market.

SPIRITUAL PRINCIPLE

Success, whether it be professional or personal, is something that nearly everyone seeks. But we all face many obstacles as we strive for it. Adversity often stands between us and our goals.

The stresses and pressures of life can make getting by difficult—and getting ahead even more so. But if we assess our situation realistically, we often find that we are doing much better than we think.

Even when we feel that we are going through life on a treadmill, constantly increasing our pace but continually seeing the same sights, we need to acknowledge that just getting on that treadmill and keeping that pace require great effort. We can then appreciate our gains, however small.

Recognize the difficulty of outperforming the market.

By accepting that obstacles will inevitably arise as we pursue our goals, we are better prepared to manage our difficulties. Otherwise, the discouragement of experiencing a setback may break our momentum. Nothing worth doing comes easily; but belief and determination can help us to achieve the measure of success that we earn through sincere effort.

Understanding that hard work and persistence are required to succeed helps us to realistically assess our progress and appreciate our gains.

Recognize the difficulty of outperforming the market.

*14. An investor
who has all the answers
doesn't even understand
the questions.*

FINANCIAL PRINCIPLE

If you think you have all the answers to investing, you are creating a formula for disappointment, if not outright failure. Even if we identify a set of investment principles, such as these, we cannot apply them to an unchanging universe of investments—or an unchanging economic or political environment. Everything is in a constant state of change.

In today's booming market, it is easy for investors, after a series of successes, to become complacent in their own knowledge and abilities. But this sense of "security" is dangerous—and false—producing a cocksure approach to investing

An investor who has all the answers doesn't even understand the questions.

that will eventually lead to disappointment, if not disaster.

Who would have predicted the economic powerhouse Japan became after World War II or the impact of the fall of communism in Russia and Eastern Europe? Investment principles are not infallible or unchangeable. They are only guidelines to follow while staying open to the changes that are inevitable.

Wise investors recognize that success is a process of continually seeking answers to new questions.

An investor who has all the answers doesn't even understand the questions.

SPIRITUAL PRINCIPLE

Life is constantly changing and producing new challenges. If we think we know all the answers, we are in a very sad state. Such a perception comes from a closed mind, which will not allow an influx of new inspiration and discoveries.

Learn to keep your mind open to new perceptions, ideas, and people with the confidence that those of value will have a positive influence. The negative influences can then fall away.

It is easy to forget the importance of preserving a child's innate sense of wonder at the world and its complexities. Albert Einstein once said that we should never lose a sense of "holy curiosity." But, unfortunately, curiosity, imagination, wonder,

An investor who has all the answers doesn't even understand the questions.

and the ability to question are too easily lost when we allow ourselves to close our minds to the wonders of the world around us.

Being open to the ever-unfolding glory and wisdom of the universe brings us to a state of humility. From this state, we can begin to realize and respect the wisdom we did not even know we had and, in the process, learn to respect the power of the universe as it manifests itself around us.

Being humble is the first step to attaining wisdom.

An investor who has all the answers doesn't even understand the questions.

15. There is
no free lunch.

FINANCIAL PRINCIPLE

This maxim covers an endless list of admonitions:

Never invest on sentiment. The company that gave you your first job or built the first car you ever owned may be a fine company. But that doesn't mean its stock is a fine investment. Even if the corporation is truly excellent, prices of its shares may be too high.

Never invest in an initial public offering (IPO) to 'save' the commission. That commission is built into the price of the stock—a reason why most new stocks decline in value after the offering. This does not mean that you should never buy an IPO. But don't buy it to save the commission.

There is no free lunch.

You can be sure that a hidden cost is larger than one that is disclosed.

Never invest solely on a tip. You might think that's obvious, and it is. But you might be surprised at how many investors, people who are well educated and successful, do exactly that. There is something psychologically compelling about a tip. Its very nature suggests inside information, a way to turn a fast profit. It very rarely is.

Even in investment, reward does not come easily—
you reap what you sow.

There is no free lunch.

Spiritual Principle

It is easy to become discouraged when hard work brings slow—or even no—progress. It is even easier to look around and envy the successes of others without understanding the effort behind those successes. Get-rich-quick schemes can seem very appealing.

Hard work, perseverance, and faith are what pay off in the long run. There are no limits to what can be achieved if you apply your talents and energies to your goals.

But there is a limit to what will be handed to you. Relationships, knowledge, wisdom, financial success—all of these things require diligent labor to cultivate and continual effort to maintain.

There is no free lunch.

Don't allow yourself to become discouraged by slow, steady gains. And don't disillusion yourself with attempts to get more than what you've earned.

The worthwhile things in life come to us through hard work, determination, and faith in our highest good.

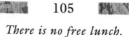

There is no free lunch.

16. Do not
be overly fearful
or negative.

FINANCIAL PRINCIPLE

For more than 100 years, optimists have carried the day in U.S. stocks. Even in the dark 1930s and 1970s, many professional money managers and many individual investors made money in stocks, especially those of smaller companies.

Of course, there will be corrections, and perhaps even crashes. But, over time, studies indicate that stocks do go up and up. With the fall of communism and the sharply reduced threat of nuclear war, it may be that free-market economies have entered the most glorious period in their history, as Sir John predicted years ago.

As national economies become more integrated and interdependent, as communication becomes

Do not be overly fearful or negative.

easier and cheaper, business is likely to boom. Trade and travel will grow. Wealth will increase. And, allowing for the inevitable corrections, stock prices should rise accordingly.

Don't allow yourself to become discouraged with minor fluctuations or losses.

Fear and negativity will erode your confidence as an investor and decrease your ability to operate successfully in the investment world.

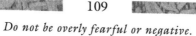

Do not be overly fearful or negative.

Spiritual Principle

Fear and negativity breed indecision and inaction. It is natural to experience these feelings on occasion. The key is not to allow ourselves to be overwhelmed by them, not to allow their shadows to pervade your life. If we approach a situation from a perspective of fear or negativity, the outcome will be affected by those feelings.

Question, consider, reflect. But in the end, to move forward, we must rely on strong spiritual truths that breed optimism and hope. Aiming high can lift us up.

The cynicism and negativity that infect many aspects of our society—the media, business community, and the law, among others—are difficult

Do not be overly fearful or negative.

to escape. It is even more crucial, then, to be a positive force in whatever you do with your life.

Temper your hopefulness with a sense of reality; but know that the light of your optimism can help improve situations and might inspire and guide others.

Optimism born of spiritual truths is the power behind growth and progress.

Do not be overly fearful or negative.

17. Those who
do good
do well.

FINANCIAL PRINCIPLE

Giving is more important than getting, and those who give freely will experience the return on their generosity. Investing for the good of humankind brings great dividends, both financially and spiritually.

Giving at least 10% of our income to charities and religious institutions is a great investment. And giving an even greater percentage of our time and energy to worthwhile causes is an investment that will pay off on many levels. As the U.S. government shifts more responsibility for the needy back to institutions and individuals, it is even more important that those who have succeeded financially develop a sense of stewardship.

Those who do good do well.

Investing financially in socially conscious funds or companies is another way to make sure that our money is performing good service. It is a little-known fact that five of the most popular 50 U.S. mutual funds—including some of the Franklin Templeton Funds—generally do not invest in tobacco, alcohol, or gambling as a matter of policy. The effects of investing without considering the potential impact of those investments on society could be detrimental and far-reaching.

An ethical investment strategy can result in financial as well as humanitarian success.

Those who do good do well.

SPIRITUAL PRINCIPLE

All of the hard work, thought, preparation, and talent you can muster may not bring real success unless helping others is part of your plan. In your work, your relationships, and your spiritual life, maintaining an attitude of "What can I give?" rather than "What can you give to me?" will bring you bountiful dividends.

Not long ago, a factory burned down, destroying a fledgling business and costing more than 100 people their jobs. The company owner was distraught over the loss of his lifetime's work; he nevertheless decided to take the insurance money from the fire and put it in a trust to guarantee his employees' salaries for six months rather than

Those who do good do well.

rebuild quickly. The result: He received many offers of capital to start over, and the business is now more successful that it was before the fire.

The gifts and talents you have been given do not belong to you. You have them on loan—in trust—to make what you can of them for the betterment of humanity. Success follows directly behind each good deed, each act of kindness and generosity. If your life on every level is led foremost by a sense of doing good, you will find yourself more satisfied with its outcomes.

What you have been given is a gift;
what you make of it will be your reward in life.

Those who do good do well.

SIR JOHN TEMPLETON

Born in 1912 in rural Winchester, Tennessee, John Marks Templeton went to Yale on a scholarship and then to Oxford University as a Rhodes scholar. An innovative investment counselor, he became a legendary figure in the financial world and a pioneer in global investing. The Templeton mutual funds have yielded billions of dollars for investors worldwide.

In 1972, he founded the Templeton Prize for Progress in Religion, the largest philanthropic monetary award in the world. Now worth more than $1 million, the Prize is given each year to someone whose work has advanced spiritual information with "striking originality," such as

Mother Teresa, Sarvepalli Radhakrishnan, Billy Graham, Aleksandr Solzhenitsyn, Charles Colson, Paul Davies, and others. In 1987, the year that Her Majesty Queen Elizabeth II knighted him for his philanthropic efforts, Sir John founded the John Templeton Foundation in Radnor, Pennsylvania.

Since retiring from the financial world in 1992, Sir John has continued to devote his time and energy to the foundation's philanthropic programs and has written and edited numerous books on science and religion.

He currently resides in Nassau, the Bahamas. ✒

A BOUT THE A UTHOR

Gary Moore was senior vice president of investments with Paine Webber before founding Gary Moore & Co.: Counsel to Ethical and Religious Investors, which provides investment counsel to banks, churches, and individuals. He also hosts a syndicated radio financial commentary program.

A member of the John Templeton Foundation advisory board, Gary is the author of several books integrating spirituality and wealth management, including *Ten Golden Rules for Financial Success: Riches I've Gathered from Legendary Mutual Fund Manager Sir John M. Templeton.*

The author lives in Sarasota, Florida with his wife, Sherry, and son, Garrett. ✎